Frank Sinatra

A Frank Sinatra Biography

Ziggy Watson

Copyright © 2017.

All rights reserved. No part of this publication may be reproduced, distributed, or transmitted in any form or by any means, including photocopying, recording, or other electronic or mechanical methods, without the prior written permission of the publisher, except in the case of brief quotations embodied in critical reviews and certain other noncommercial uses permitted by copyright law.

This book is intended for informational and entertainment purposes only. The publisher limits all liability arising from this work to the fullest extent of the law.

Table of Contents

Introduction

Early Years

Getting Started in the Big City

Dabbling in Big Bands

The Bobby-Soxers

Live at the Paramount

Career Slump, The Rat Pack, and Revival

The End of an Era

Introduction

"If nothing survived of Sinatra but what's been written about him, posterity would have a hugely misleading impression. If you had never heard the music and only read the biographies (or seen the documentaries with the sound off), you'd be left with a sense of bigness: big voice, big manner, big entertainer — a brawling guy, a sort of pop Pavarotti, a crooner Caruso, a guy blessed with a giant instrument that sets plaster falling from the ceiling, but who didn't use his instrument well or have much taste.

--Adam Gopnik, The New Yorker, 2015'

Frank Sinatra is the 20th century's greatest male singer and it's not particularly close. His relaxed and easy performance style mixed with his famous wit has made him a household name worldwide, some 50 years after his peak. There are few that can hold a candle to him and even fewer that try. His imitators are numerous and his influence is unavoidable. This is the story of a young Italian boy living in New Jersey who dreamed of something bigger and had the gumption to do out and get it.

There are surely competitors. Bing Crosby, in particular, was the man that inspired Sinatra to become a singer in the first place. But Sinatra was talented enough to take what Crosby laid out and grow from it — creating something that had never been seen before. Sinatra did all this without any formal training in music and without the virtuosity that was seemingly necessary before his rise. That's not to say his work wasn't complex or meaningful, on the contrary, the emotion that he offered for the pieces he sang could be felt in every syllable.

Above all, he had a voice. But, he also lived a life that was his own and made sure everyone knew it. He was an iconic musical figure in three different decades. He was Frank Sinatra. Sinatra lived a life of relative wonder upon being discovered as a part of a jazz group in the 1940's. But Frank was always one to stand out of the group. There were other singers in his contemporary periods that had more talent, more natural ability. But there was no one who had the draw quite like Sinatra.

Sinatra was the complete package when it came to the art of crooning. He looked best when he had lowball glass of whiskey in one hand and a microphone in the other. This mysterious, Byronic attraction made him a superstar early on and then gave his career the legs it needed to make him a legend. The teeny boppers and bobby-soxers (teenage girls) were his first fans, but over the years, every part of American culture has been affected by Frank Sinatra, especially jazz and pop music.

However, his life didn't start out the way you might have expected. He came from nothing and nobody to be something. His mother dressed him in the nicest suits while going through hard times and good times. He was a man of the people first and foremost—and it came out in his music. Especially later, when Frank's life became a collage of the finest life American fame had to offer, Frank could still sing about the hardships and intrigues of the average person. His heartbreak was always your heartbreak too.

Most of the time, in those days, the music was not written or composed by the singer or the band. There were typically dedicated songwriters who wrote for multiple acts and all had their own reputations. Frank could take the music from these freelance writers and make it sound like something he had written in his own living room and sung from the heart to close friends.

As his daughter, Nancy Sinatra would say, "Everyone description of my father includes the word: 'American'." She was not wrong. His particular style of brooding, nervous masculinity became the hallmark of the American male in the modern era. Think about his features that are now associated with tough, respectable, American men: the immaculate suits, the dapper derby hat tilted to one side, the budding alcoholism, the ability to be the life of the party, and of course the sensation that he was connected to every living person that could be called important.

However, there was always an aspect of his personality that was larger-than-life, untouchable. Sinatra wasn't some follower of a doctrine or the patsy to a passing fad, he was the trend-setter. Much of that is expressed in his song, My Way:

I've lived a life that's full
I've traveled each and every highway
But much more than this
I did it my way

Regrets, I've had a few
But then again, too few to mention
I did what I had to do
And I saw it through without exemption

I planned each charted course
Each careful step along the byway
And much, much more than this
I did it my way

This song is a perfect representation of Sinatra's personality, though he didn't write the lyrics. This was a time of stunning hardship and even more incredible responses to adversity and he was no exception. But despite all of that, he was still glamorous and regal and unique.

His persona was likely derived from his experience as the only child to a pair of hard-working Italian immigrants. Later, his background would make him something of an icon in the immigrant community. He was given every advantage his parents could afford and his mother pushed him to become the best he could be in the land of opportunity—despite her harsh ways and their deep philosophical differences.

In the end, Sinatra sold 150 million records worldwide, proving two distinct facts: The United States became the dominant cultural force during the 1940s (with its radio, tv, and musical artists at the helm) and that Sinatra was chief among them. Not only that, but Sinatra could claim that he had a part in the success of all the major mediums of the era—film, television, and of course, music/radio.

Sinatra took the best parts of growing up an immigrant in the United States and made something of them. He is a prime example of the type of success that was found when America opened its doors to those that needed its help. The country is continually enriched by the Italian-Americans, Irish-Americans, African-Americans and so forth.

He retained his hard-working passion through most of his life, refusing to record unless it was live and with a band, poring over every bit of music he could lay hands on (although he never learned to read tablature), and performing well into his advanced age--and in any way you could imagine.

When you think of the 40s, 50s, and 60s, we may not all see the same thing. But, somewhere, off in the distance of your mind's eye is the soft tones of a Sinatra ballad. There is no extricating him from the period because he defined the period, itself. The Story of Frank Sinatra begins here, but it will likely echo off American skyrises for centuries to come.

Early Years

My father almost died the day he was born. He came into the world fighting for his life. He was thirteen and a half pounds at birth, a big baby lodged inside a tiny woman, less than five feet tall. The doctor had trouble getting him out. The doctor tugged away with forceps, ripping the baby's ear, cheek and neck, and producing scars he would always carry. The newborn did not breathe. Thinking him dead, the doctor turned instead to treat the mother. The baby's grandmother scooped him up and held him under running water. Life.

--Nancy Sinatra

Sinatra would win his first fight. It is the most simple fight a person can be involved in. He simply wanted to live. His daughter, quoted here, believed that this was the moment that gave him the fighting spirit he would be famous for in life, the stage, and the screen. He tasted the edge of death so early in his life that adversity became a bone in his body. As a baby, Sinatra would become a fighter. He would need this grit for the rest of his life, starting with the relationship he had with his mother. An immigrant businesswoman, nurse, and politician, his mother tested him daily for his entire life. She would be the defining parental influence for him and their relationship began with a brush with death.

Frank Sinatra had an inauspicious beginning to his life like many other immigrants to America in the 20th century. His parents, of full Italian origin, brought their hopes and dreams to the United States and had just one child: Frank Sinatra. Dolly Sinatra and Antonino "Marty"

Sinatra were married at the city hall in New Jersey a couple of years before and led a very tight, lower income lifestyle.

Frank, however, was quite a bit different than the other children in his neighborhood. First of all, he retained the scars of his violent birth for his entire life. His stout Roman Catholic parents had to wait three months to christen their son due to the open wounds still marring his body. Ironically, perhaps, Sinatra's eardrum was busted by the forceps, as well. For a legendary musician, Sinatra had a terrible start to his life. It's unlikely anyone expected he would someday make the world wilt with his world-class tone.

Sinatra wasn't just held back by the scars from his birth, he also had to deal with years of cystic acne. With welts covering his face for most of his puberty days, he was lucky to have made it to Hollywood with a face that people wanted to see. Sinatra blamed his looks on the doctor that delivered him, who may or may not have given up on a baby way too early, and often wished he could have punched him in the mouth. Even worse, the kids called him "Scarface" and derided him at every opportunity.

Life at home wasn't exactly easy, either. His mother, Dolly was about as headstrong as it was possible for her to be in the circles the Sinatra's frequented. Dolly was active in politics, social issues, and most importantly: Frank's life. As their only child, the pressure was on Frank to become something more. Dolly was shipped off to the United States before her first birthday and was born-and-raised as a hard-nosed immigrant. She pushed Frank constantly throughout his childhood.

Nancy Sinatra remembers how her father described his upbringing, "They'd fought through his childhood and continued to do so until her dying day. But I believe that to counter her steel will he'd developed his own. To prove her wrong when she belittled his choice of career... Their friction first had shaped him; that, I think, had remained to the end and a litmus test of the grit in his bones. It helped keep him at the top of his game."

In a lot of ways, experiences like his serve to hasten an individual's maturity and experience. Sinatra was constantly in a world of his own creation, with no real mooring in an experience that anyone had ever felt before. Yet, he was able to continually succeed. There is always something to be said for adaptability.

Sinatra's father, a slight man from Sicily, had spent less time in the States than his wife but was no less hardened by the experience. Known as "Marty" professionally, Antonino would box for 2 decades. At the time, it was somewhat common for a blue-collar worker to moonlight as an amateur/professional boxer. The movie "Cinderella Man" was about the true story of a similar boxer who was forced to work the docks as an out of work boxer.

Marty was only "Marty" because, in an effort to fit into New York City in the early twentieth century, he changed his name to Marty O'Brien. This helped him draw people into his matches because, for some reason, it was more popular to be Irish than Italian at the time.

Marty was never able to find much success boxing, but he was able to keep food on his family's table between that and the work he did at various factories and at the New Jersey/New York City docks. He eventually had to retire after breaking both of his wrists boxing and finally found work at a fire department — though he would suffer asthma and lung problems for the rest of his life thanks to subpar working conditions.

Nancy Sinatra recalls her father saying, "He inhaled that dust [from the factory] for seventeen years and it wrecked his lungs. He couldn't do any better because he had nobody to teach him English."

Marty and Dolly were never the types to follow the rules too closely, and that certainly rubbed off on Frank eventually. His parents, with a five-year-old in tow, started a tavern that was illegally selling alcohol to people in their community during the time of prohibition. There wasn't much worry about the law taking action against them, as many law enforcement officers refused to enforce prohibition. It has also been speculated that the there were an element of the Italian mob at play, with many offering conjectures that there were criminal elements that assisted the Sinatra's and their early business.

Either way, Dolly Sinatra was going to find some way to end up on the wrong side of someone. She was a huge factor in her community when it came to getting votes for the Democratic party. She was eventually elected to a position as the first woman ever to hold it. In her spare time, she would chain herself to municipal buildings as a show of support for women's suffrage. A biographer for Sinatra later stated that she had also run a makeshift abortion clinic for her neighborhood—a story supported by her career as a midwife.

In any event, Sinatra was known for having a good life in those days. He was an only child, so his parents could afford more costly items for him. His style of dress was always impeccable, thanks to his extensive collection of clothing purchased by his mother, and he even had his own room—unheard of during the Great Depression in the urban sprawl. His youth was spent singing songs on the corner and doing homework beneath the din of tavern music and merriment.

As nice as that may sound, Sinatra would still clash with his mother—who was often too busy to really get to know her own son. He became entranced with the popular big band music of the time. He learned early that it was great to earn attention and cash by entertaining his friends and family. Saying, "One day, I got a nickel. I said, 'This is the racket'. I thought, "It's wonderful to sing…I never forgot it."

Frank's aspirations were likely spurred on by his father's short career in show business that started with Marty taking parts as extras in some early films set in the area. He never found any success from that industry and he and his wife considered it a dead end. When they found out that Frank wanted to pursue a career in that area, they were prohibitive and upset. Marty was insistent that his son does not become a "bum" and that he gets a more practical job.

Nancy would remark on Frank's changing relationship with his mother and father, particularly his mother, "They'd fought through his childhood and continued to do so until her dying day. But I believe that to counter her steel will he'd developed his own. To prove her wrong when she belittled his choice of career … Their friction first had shaped him; that, I think, had remained to the end and a litmus test of the grit in his bones. It helped keep him at the top of his game."

This was further complicated when Frank was expelled from high school after less than 2 months of attendance. He was a rowdy kid and got into trouble more often than not. It seemed that the school systems of the day had no room for him. So now, Frank was left with fewer options than before. His parents were mortified and it seemed that, with every passing day, the heat was turned up on him.

Most of this was applied by his mother, who was very active in her community and harbored big dreams—just ones that began a little closer to home. The relationship troubles between Frank and his mother didn't begin with this disagreement, but they were certainly exacerbated by it. There are many stories from Frank's childhood that beatings he took from his mother, whom he mirrored in his tenacity and stubbornness. Despite Dolly's misgivings about Frank's choices, she created someone who was just like her. She should have known that this was going to happen, really.

The best example of the panache that Frank inherited from his mother is, in fact, his own birth. Dolly's family was from a wealthier area in Italy that was known for lithography (early printing) and literature. Frank's father came from Sicily, where they are farmers and are typically grape-growers. There was an uproar when Dolly announced she was marrying someone below her class, but she did it anyway.

As Nancy would later write, "Dolly and Marty met when they were kids, and Grandma's parents opposed the romance. Marty's parents were Sicilian, they were grape growers. Dolly's parents were Genovese, they were lithographers, and there was a class distinction between the families. But Dolly was a very aggressive girl, very strong-minded, and she did what she wanted to do."

Thus, Frank's years as a child in New Jersey, Hoboken to be exact, were fraught with adversity but not short on love. His upbringing was closely aligned with the story of many immigrants from that period, although Frank was born-and-bred American. He would later use this experience to come away as one of the greatest figures in Italian American culture and an icon to those who were going through the same thing.

Getting Started in the Big City

"On my night off, Monday, I would go to wherever there was a big band playing around New York and I'd just stand at the bandstand, like kids used to do. And I saw all the good bands and then I saw [Tommy] Dorsey. I thought to myself, 'That's the band to be with…"

--Frank Sinatra, Frank Sinatra: My Father

After his early childhood career of being the local saloon boy, Sinatra was hooked on the idea of singing for a living. As a young boy, he was also committed to the process that would get him there. He began to work on his voice regularly, as a hobby and later as a professional practice. He, like many other future musicians and singers, sung along to the radio and recordings of his favorite artists like Bing Crosby and Gene Autry.

This time is notable for the many legendary acts that never really knew how to read or write music tablature. Sinatra was definitely one of them. However, thanks to improvement in communication technology like the radio and the record player, people could learn music by ear. This was a game-changer that allowed people like Frank to enter the world of music if they had talent — and less so because he was able to take the time to learn musical notation.

He would even start taking elocution lessons from a teacher in the city. He did this to improve his speech and pronunciation in order to help his career and spur more mainstream appeal than his background might have allowed at the time. However, his vocal coach noticed his impressive range and encourage Sinatra to continue his quest to become a professional.

Around his 20th birthday, his mother was able to procure him a spot on a genial local group, the 3 Flashes. They would later state that Frank was only allowed to join because he owned a car and could give them rides. Sinatra, however, was in awe of them. He was amazed that people he knew could work their voice boxes for a living. Once he was in the group, they renamed themselves the Hoboken Four and auditioned for an amateur singing contest that was televised. They won this contest, likely setting forth a series of events that would end with Sinatra being one of the world's most celebrated talents.

But first, there was the matter of the contest. Once they won, they were gifted a 6-month contract that put them on stages and radios across the country. Frank quickly became the face of the group, since, although he had scarring and cystic acne, he was the most attractive to the girls that became quick fans. They were so popular that the amateur singing contest kept inviting them back to win it under different pseudonyms and monikers to keep ratings high.

This was still not enough to get him over the hump. His group was successful, but they were outnumbered. There was a glut of acts at the time that kept Frank from making any real waves, especially as the country leaped from the Depression to all-out war.

He would take odd jobs along the way. He worked as a boilermaker, a riveter, and a delivery boy. At one point, before he started singing, he even attended a business school. This one lasted longer than 2 months, but he was gone again before the year was out. In another case, he was a lifeguard for a nearby beach. It was here that he would meet the mother of his daughter, Nancy, whom he conceived out of wedlock.

Frank had a few girls at the time and it all came to a head when Nancy's mother showed up to the beach to tell him she was pregnant. Frank, who was there with another girl, was dumbfounded. His current beau attacked the pregnant girl and Frank was forced to intervene. He stated clearly that he was going to do the right thing and marry this girl so that the child would not be a bastard and her life wouldn't be ruined. An inauspicious start to Nancy's life to be sure, but it runs in the family.

In his career, he seemed to be taking steps backward. 3 years after his success on television, he was back working as a singing waiter for $15 an hour. Life changes quickly in the big city. Frank would continue to make his way, however. He could be found at various clubs and bars in the Hoboken area, performing for paltry sums. Some days he would simply sing for money and cigarettes on the street. There is a small segment of the New Jersey population that saw Sinatra live before anyone would even charge a gate fee.

His gig with the singing restaurant turned out to be bigger than others might have expected. Sinatra was adamant that it was his big break, thanks to strong connections to the joint and a local radio station. This gave him enough clout to get a group together on a show called Dance Parade. Sinatra was right, he was soon spotted by a made saxophone player named Frank Mane. Mane set him up with his first audition for a recording. This would turn out to be Our Love, a song written as a love letter to classical music. It was based off Romeo and Juliet. While not getting the huge acclaim that would come later, this recording got him noticed by a few other acts that would turn out to be influential in his life.

The first of these was to be Harry James, one of the same big band leaders that entranced young Sinatra on the streets of New York. He would make huge inroads with him, joining the band immediately after recording Our Love. Frank was finally on his way.

Dabbling in Big Bands

It would be nice to say that when Frank got his first big break, he would need no more—that he was a made man. However, that's not how this story begins. The road to stardom is never a straight path and there was much that needed to happen before Frank would ever get a chance to show the nation what he was made of. He was a big fish, but he was a big fish in an ocean—not a pond. He needed something to set him apart: the voice. Here's how he got it, by firsthand account from Nancy and Frank Sinatra:

Frank: "In those days, working with a big band was the end of the rainbow for any singer who wanted to make it."

He heard that respected trumpet player Harry James was leaving Benny Goodman [a local big band] to start a band of his own. Nancy [Sinatra's wife and Nancy's mother] got a fifteen-dollar advance on her salary so she could have publicity pictures taken to give to Harry James."

The recordings Sinatra had completed earlier had been heard by James before they had ever met. James, intrigued, traveled to the singing restaurant, The Rustic Cabin, and listened to him sing with the band there. He sang "Begin the Beguine" and James made his decision. He hired Sinatra to become a featured singer in his band.

This break couldn't have come at a better time. Nancy Barbato, the same girl who was assaulted when she told Frank she was pregnant with his child, was doing her best to make a home for the young couple. There were times when money was tight and it seemed like the whole world was pressing down on them, but they made it through. Lacking the money to make anything out of their marriage, they were forced to take their honeymoon at home and spent the time making their apartment habitable.

Not just that, but Frank's tenure at The Rustic Cabin wasn't going as well as he would have liked. He had such self-assured way about him that he would continually rub his struggling coworkers the wrong way. He faced derision and ostracization at every turn until he could hustle a contract with Harry James and his band.

The contract was for 2 years at a rate of $75 a week. Sinatra was over the moon, he was finally able to provide for his fledgling family and stick with one act, instead of traveling hundreds of miles for work like he had been. With all the training he received from his time as an amateur, plus his new ability to expand his vocal range to the more traditional jazz ranges, Frank was ready to hit it big.

It is around this time that the ties Sinatra had with the mob began to show themselves, at least within the retrospective provided by the passing time. Sinatra's mother was part of a well-respected family that had clout with some of the American mobsters that inhabited New York and New Jersey. It is said that Frank's audition with Harry James was set up because Frank performed well for some of the most influential mob bosses at the time. Either way, it was time to hit the road.

It was a hard road with the Harry James band, they were never really able to get anything off the ground. James had been attracted to Sinatra's moxie and his ability to "talk a lyric." But none of his abilities could make the success of the band seem achievable. Frank wanted to be a part of something that would change his life.

Unfortunately, that change came too slowly. Frank released his first real single in, "From the Bottom of My Heart" but it sold less than ten thousand copies. He began to feel frustrated, even though the experience he was getting was building him into a star. He started to look around at other bands to see if he could find a way to up his standing.

This opportunity came, as you might have guessed. It came in the form of the Tommy Dorsey band that Sinatra had heaped praise upon in the previous section. Their lead singer was on the outs and Sinatra jumped at the idea of being able to sing lead in one of his favorite bands and his biggest chance yet.

Frank was known in Dorsey's circles thanks to his interest in a gentleman named Bob Chester. Chester was able to get Frank an audition with Dorsey at a local club and Frank nailed it. Soon enough, he was going to be playing in the band that had his eye from the very beginning. He believed Dorsey was the exact kind of person that could help him become the entertainer he knew he could be.

There was still the matter of Sinatra's other band. Harry James was saddened but not vindictive, he allowed Sinatra to get out of his contract as long as he could find a replacement. Once that was done, there was nothing left to do but leave. At the final show in Buffalo, New York, Frank described his uncertainty:

"That was the last gig I had with James and I was going home to spend some time with Nancy and she was to meet me at the train the next morning and the band was going to Hartford to do a one-nighter…It was rather like 'Death of a Salesman' in the snow as I stood there with my two bags and the bus was pulling away and I had lived with those guys and they were fun and I stood there like a schmuck and I'm in tears as I see the red lights going away. And the snow's coming down and I figure to myself I ain't never gonna make it, and I'll never get home and it'll be terrible, I'm going to die up here in the Buffalo snow"

Frank was in the band. He was so excited that he didn't even ask about the details of his position. When he told his wife, she said, "That means you'll be getting more money." However, Frank had never asked how much he would be paid. It was an afterthought. He replied, "I don't know, I was just so happy to get a job." His pay had, in fact, increased to $100 a week. That adds up to something like $1500 a week in 2017 money.

Despite his earlier misgivings, Sinatra was excitedly nervous to begin his career with Dorsey and his band. They performed in a suburb of Chicago and Dorsey later recalled, "You could almost feel the excitement coming up out of the crowds when the kid stood up to sing. Remember, he was no matinee idol. He was just a skinny kid with big ears. I used to stand there so amazed I'd almost forget to take my own solos."

This would come as a surprise because of the massive cold shoulder that was delivered to Sinatra from the members of the band that were less than thrilled to see their lead singer left. He went from being in a group of equals to being the underling that must prove himself. It's safe to say that it worked out in the end.

He complained that the other members of the band wouldn't give him the time of day to his wife. Then, he decided to ignore them and play his own game. Sinatra began to develop what he would call a "method of long phraseology" and, with every passing day, he inspired more confidence from his fellow members. It was if a switch had clicked with Sinatra. Again, the adversity of a situation brought out the best in the "ol' Blue Eyes."

Dorsey was able to recognize Sinatra's talent in a way that no one else had been able to and he was rewarded handsomely for it. Dorsey would take on a fatherly role to Frank, whose own father had tossed him out of the house for failing high school and wanting to sing. Frank fell in line with Dorsey and began to copy everything that he could, down to mannerisms and even Dorsey's model trains.

The hard work paid off and eventually, Sinatra was able to record something that actually made it onto the charts, in the form of a ditty called Polka Dots and Moonbeams. It was a song very much in the style of the traditional Bing Crosby tone that was the most popular way of singing at the time. But, for the first time, you could tell you were dealing with something different.

One of Sinatra's bandmates, Jo Stafford would remember sitting on the bandstand as Sinatra made his debut performance. Sinatra was slim and had long hair — acceptable, but just outside the norms of the time. He struck an imposing figure. Still, Stafford and his mates were unenthused about the man who had replaced their lead singer. Until he actually sang. They were all struck at how unique Sinatra's style and approach was, the ease of which he delivered lines. The biggest surprise? He made no attempt to sound like Bing Crosby. Sinatra was in.

The Bobby-Soxers

In American society, there is a success when a business, person, or product fills a need that nobody else realized needed to be filled. Sinatra found his success in the teenage girls of that era, known as "bobby-soxers". Before the Beatles and the Rolling Stones came to America and induced hours of constant screaming and occasional fainting in the teenage girl, Sinatra had a hold of that market that was the envy of every entertainer in the business. The Beatles would eventually eschew this popularity because they believed their music suffered under the weight of the fandom and the noise. Sinatra suffered no such anxieties because once you're in, you're in.

In 1940, Sinatra was playing songs for pennies for an unknown and some unknown club. By

1945, there was no bigger star in the United States. The story of how this happened isn't particularly hard to imagine, but it is nonetheless fascinating. When the rubber met the road with Sinatra, it seemed his personality just grew larger and surer of itself. By 1945, they were writing articles about Sinatra that declared he was the eye in a hurricane of mass hysteria. Thousands of young people rushed to absorb anything they could that he was a part of. Whatever Sinatra touched was a gold mine for any entertainer, publicist, or producer. With the advent of this new generation of teens, there was someone to capitalize in a way the world will never forget. Young girls in their teens were the target and there hadn't been someone so successful with that demographic since the escapades of Lindbergh earlier in the century.

There are many answers about why he became as big as he did, but there is no doubt that his fame exploded in a period of 2-3 years. The same Sinatra that was singing happy songs to passers-by on the street corner was now selling out every venue by himself---as a solo act.

At the height of Sinatramania, Frank couldn't appear in public without an entourage of armed policemen and he attracted enormous attention everywhere he went. A well-publicized event had him show up at the campaign rally for the rival of President Franklin Delano Roosevelt. Sinatra, an ardent supporter of the famous New York Governor and Democrat, claimed he was merely attending the event.

Though, some have suggested that there was more ill will to his appearance that may have met the eye. Sinatra's presence completely halted the proceedings and the rally had to be canceled for fear of further disturbance. Politics was always a part of Sinatra's life, and as you will see, his immense fame only made this more of a reality.

His fame would only be rivaled by the later appearances of Elvis and The Beatles, but remember, they were big because they were on TV all the time. Sinatra had no such luck, radio was still king. He had to do it on his own, with just his voice and a nice suit. Unlike in our current media culture, there were a negligible amount of people who had ever actually seen him, first hand. His films had yet to take off and his TV appearances were not yet numerous enough to have much effect. Still, his voice drew people into him like none other of his era.

There were stages during the 40's when the fashion statement preferred by teenagers was to copy Frank Sinatra at every turn. If he wore certain kind of tie, you can be certain that it would be a popular item in the coming weeks. His polka-dotted tie fetish caught on, in fact, and became a hot style for some time—in an era of somber masculinity. The bobby-soxers, named for their propensity to wear knee-high white socks instead of stockings like their mothers, were entranced.

There were bobby-soxers before Sinatra, but now nobody remembers them for anything except their undying love for Sinatra and the crooners of the age. However, there were none that possessed the level of attraction Sinatra demanded. He was only able to reach these heights as a solo act, a journey that ended one of the most important relationships in his life.

After joining Tommy Dorsey's band, Sinatra found some success as the lead singer. But nothing had prepared him for how good he sounded in his recordings. Something must have clicked for Frank in those days because he became assured of his own success. The straw that broke the camel's back, however, were recordings of Frank during a stand in Hollywood. From that point on, he was set on becoming a solo act—and he was going after Bing Crosby, the biggest act of them all.

There was a bit of a snag, however. When Sinatra had signed with Tommy Dorsey, he never really looked at the contract in a real way. When it came time for him to move on—he found out that Dorsey had a claim to 43 percent of all of Sinatra's future earnings as an entertainer. Frank was, naturally, livid. He demanded that he be released from this unfair deal and given a chance to shine on his own.

Dorsey was obviously in on the whole thing, considering he signed Sinatra to that contract in the first place. Despite how much Frank looked up to him, Dorsey wanted to own him. That just wasn't going to work for the skinny Italian kid from New Jersey. Sinatra sued Dorsey and the legal battle lasted a full year. During that time Sinatra's relationship with Dorsey was completely sullied and it never fully recovered.

When the suit was eventually settled out of court, Sinatra agreed to pay a few thousand dollars for the right to own his work. It was a stupid deal signed by an awestruck kid and he certainly paid for it. What is less certain, however, is how Frank was able to convince him that it was in his best interests to do so.

There is a rumor that a mobster connected to the Sinatra's ambushed Dorsey and forced him out of the contract. He was said to have done so by holding a gun to Dorsey's head and forcing him to promise to end the case. Whatever happened in the end, Sinatra made moves that would put him on top and using Dorsey's band as a catapult into stardom was his first act. When Dorsey died in 1956, Sinatra wasn't there and there was never any resolution. Dorsey would say before his death, "He's the most fascinating man in the world, but don't put your hand in the cage."

If you remember what was said about Sinatra finding a market and a product that no one knew existed, this was the moment that come to fruition. In the early 1940's there came a new kind of teenage girl, one that was allowed and able to appreciate music and the men and women who performed it. All the sudden, there was a huge population of fans that came from nowhere.

Although it may be stereotypical of me to say, there is definitive proof that these girls wanted to listen to hot, young, male performers more than anything. The music business, a very adult enterprise at the time, was designed to be slow moving and safe for the pleasure of those who were old enough to know what they wanted. This new kind of fan demanded more, they wanted something with panache. Guess who had that in spades?

Sinatra was already topping the reader's polls in magazines left and right for the favorite male performer. By the time he was ready to go solo, he exploded in a way that no one had really anticipated.

As Frank would later say, "I think my appeal was due to the fact that there hadn't been a troubadour around for ten or twenty years, from the time that Bing had broken in and went on to radio and movies. And he, strangely enough, had appealed primarily to older people, middle-aged people.

But, as Sinatra would notice, the young people in America didn't seem to have anybody singing for them. When he came around, it was a cultural zeitgeist, in part because he arrived at the exact right time. And, also, because of the immense talent he brought to the table when he did arrive. Sinatra didn't know what role he was to play, but he felt that it was important, that spirit drove him for the rest of his career.

The time had come to see what Frank was made of, and there was little left in his way.

Would he finally be able to live up to the expectations that he had set for himself? Sinatra decided the best way to know was to set up a solo show at the same theater that inspired him to go solo in the first place: Paramount Theatre in New York City.

Live at the Paramount

"I was in New York City doing a radio show, and Bob Weitman, who ran the Paramount, came to me and asked if just before I do my radio show, I could come over to the Paramount for the debut of Frank Sinatra. I said, 'Who?" He said, "Frank Sinatra, and Benny Goodman's Orchestra…So, I said, "Well, who the hell is Frank Sinatra?" And he said to me, "You mean to tell me that you have never heard of Frank Sinatra?" I said, "No." He said, "Well, he is the hottest thing in the country right now." I said, "I'm sorry, but I never heard of him. But, Bob, I'll do this for you and Benny Goodman and Sinatra too if it is any help."

---Comedian Jack Benny on Sinatra's Opening Night

The time had come for Sinatra to open as a solo act. As Jack Benny references here, there was still a large portion of adult entertainers that had no idea who Frank Sinatra was. For the most part, his acclaim had been limited to teen publications and marketing, since he fared so well in that arena. However, after this night, there would no longer be any excuse to ignore him. Here's more from Benny as he navigates this strange, life-changing night from his first-hand perspective:

"So, I go there, I'm backstage with Benny Goodman, waiting to be introduced, and Bob Weitman was there, and they introduced me to this skinny little kid called Frank Sinatra. Now it's time for the introductions, and first Benny Goodman went on and did his act, and then he says, "Now, ladies and gentlemen, to introduce our honored guest, we have Jack Benny." So I walked out on a little ramp and got a very nice reception, you know, I thought it was nice, I certainly didn't think Sinatra would get much of anything because I never heard of him."

These were the moments right before Benny introduced Sinatra to the world as a solo act. Jack Benny was a class act, but there is definitely some humor to be found in his ignorance and ambivalence towards this new "star." Although it was clear Benny had his doubts, he recalls a pleasant meeting with a very relaxed Sinatra beforehand. Nothing that had happened thus far could have prepared Benny for the reception Sinatra was about to receive.

Jack Benny, the pro that he was, introduced Sinatra as if he had known him for years. Of course, this was all an act. For all Benny knew, this was some nobody he needed his help to get off the ground. His expectations for Sinatra's reception were, thus, understandably low. But when he said, "Well, anyway, ladies and gentlemen, here he is, Frank Sinatra!" the roar from the crowd became overwhelming.

Benny had never heard anything like it. He was shaken as it seemed that the theatre was going to burst from all of the excitement. There were girls screaming as if they had been murdered and people of all ages rushing down the aisles for a chance to get next to the bandstand. It was absolute pandemonium — and Benny had never heard of him.

The world was about to hear from him, especially after the tremendous success that was to be Sinatra's coming-out party. Sinatra, himself, remarked, "The sound that greeted me was absolutely deafening. It was a tremendous roar. Five thousand kids, stamping, yelling, screaming, applauding. I was scared stiff. I couldn't move a muscle. Benny Goodman froze, too. He was so scared he turned around, looked at the audience, and said, 'What the hell is that?' I burst out laughing."

His show was held on the December 30th, 1942, and that was the last year that the world was unaware of Frank Sinatra. He would go on to perform at the Paramount for 8 weeks after this show, double the maximum of his original contract with Weitman. Even without the extra shows, the damage had been done. There were more Sinatra fan clubs in the next few weeks than there had been Sinatra fans before his debut.

You might have heard the term "Beatlemania" to describe the absolute insanity that followed the debut of the legendary British group to the United States and abroad. However, they were not the first. "Sinatramania" was a coined two decades before that due to his massive popularity with the bobby-soxers and teenagers all around.

Much like the Beatles after him, the fame nearly reached dangerous levels. In 1944, at yet another Paramount Theatre performance, nearly 35,000 fans rioted outside of the show because there was not nearly enough room. There were only 250 people that were allowed in. The riot was so bad, they named it the Columbus Day Riot and it changed how Sinatra perceived his fans and fame.

His personality was perfect for this newfound role, however. He had always been the kind of person to act cool and collected, no matter what. People, especially young girls, were attracted to his laid-back attitude and his young looks. His manager cultivated a persona that emphasized his immigrant roots and his humble upbringing. Girls everywhere saw someone who they thought might understand, might try to fall in love with them. This new age of female fandom would have a marked effect on what type of performers would be stars in the coming years.

Previously, the only people that were buying records were married people and adults that listened to music as an escape—often from the rigors of parenthood. However, the teenage factor was immediately apparent in Sinatra's rise to fame. His voice kept him on top, but his appeal to the younger and fairer sex put him there. By the beginning of 1943, he had completely overtaken the other most popular male performers of his time, even Bing Crosby.

Record companies were, obviously, very interested in capitalizing on his fame. Sinatra signed a deal with Columbia Records and they set to work on his future immediately. The first thing they did was release some old Sinatra singles from his time with Harry James and his band. There was already a wealth of recordings from his pre-fame days that fans would eat up, regardless. He released "All or Nothing at All" and it charted the very next day, staying up for 18 weeks as a best seller. However, Columbia knew that its best bet was to create as much new music as possible. So, they set out to create a new Sinatra discography that would elevate him to new levels.

Over the course of several months, Sinatra recorded 9 songs, of which 7 were best-sellers. The next order of business for Sinatra was to show the world that he was no longer a nobody. He began playing concerts to high-society landmarks, like the legendary hotel The Waldorf Astoria in New York City. Finally, those lights that a young Sinatra had seen from across the Hudson were his to see.

There would be more to talk about from this era if the world, itself, had not started to fall apart at the same time. World War II broke out in America after years on the sidelines. Sinatramania was put on the backburner as everyone prepared for one of the most horrific examples of warfare ever perpetrated. The attack on Pearl Harbor had rendered any anti-war statements moot and the United States began work on the atomic bomb that would end up finishing the war.

Sinatra was, by no means, ignorant of the stakes in the current political situation. He was the son of a prominent Democrat and community organizer: Dolly Sinatra. He knew what he was talking about and regularly inserted himself into political discussions, gladly using his fame to add weight to causes that he believed in. In particular, he was an early proponent of President Franklin Delano Roosevelt and a staunch supporter of his war efforts.

Roosevelt, a New York elite, had been governor during the young years of Sinatra's young manhood and that played a large part in allocating support amongst immigrant populations that were mostly concentrated in the big cities of the northeast. Despite his early support of the Democratic Party, Sinatra would eventually pay tribute to many different sitting presidents—even Ronald Reagan, who was about as far from FDR as a man could get.

Sinatra was of the age to be drafted at the time of its statement and was forced to go to a recruitment station and submit to a physical. This is another area where the details become fuzzy due to the age of this story. There are several explanations for why Sinatra did not join the army—but before any of those are given—understand that it is very likely that Sinatra did much more work for the USO and troop confidence than he would have done as a skinny, unwilling soldier.

Sinatra was given a 4-F designation upon the conclusion of his physical, which meant that he would not be required to join the military through the draft. The official reasoning for this was that he could not be admitted due to his "perforated eardrum." Regardless if this is an excuse or not, there is some definite proof that his difficult birth was a factor throughout his life.

However, once the dust had settled in the war, it came to light that the actual army records of his examination complained of what they called "emotional instability." This raises several questions, especially about what sort of instability he showed during his brief time with the recruiters.

Another competing theory is that he was withheld due to hypertension. This is the typical reasoning for his luck in war. It was even said that it was demanded he stay in their facilities for a few days so that they could personally test his hypertension. As excuses go, this is a much better option and it doesn't baffle anyone that his family would prefer this story—not to mention it's a much better reason to miss the war entirely than some easy-to-cover-up ear issues.

Darker still, there is the persisting idea that the mob once again helped him out of a bind and gave him an out in the military. There is no doubt that the mafia would be able to pull something like that off, so if he was able and willing to sing it, it was a possible option. A columnist even once reported that he had paid $40,000 to avoid service—through subsequent investigation by the FBI would render this assertion baseless.

Sinatra, for better or worse, spent much of wartime doing shows for USO efforts and other military-minded pursuits and benefits. Most of the working actors and singers that were spared a cold, hard trip to Europe or the Pacific theater spent their time trying to make the people that were here feel better about their plight.

Sinatra would work constantly for the next few years, raking in the money and fame like nobody else around. But, his career was entering a different period — the world was changing and Sinatra would have to change to go along with it. The adoration of bobby-soxers would only go so far to accomplish his dreams. Sinatra was ready to turn another page.

Career Slump, The Rat Pack, and Revival

"The president is dead," the radio announcer said. I was only four, but there is no misunderstanding those four words. FDR—gone. Harry Truman, Hiroshima, and Nagasaki. The times were changing. The bobby-soxers were growing up, and Frank Sinatra was on top. And he was doing his part, touring for the USO, and was beginning to adjust to the loss of the president."

--Nancy Sinatra, Frank Sinatra: My Father

Indeed, things were changing and they were changing rapidly. As fortuitous as his early success was, there was little chance that he would be able to keep it up forever. The workload, the expectations, and the fandom were downright insane and it would change Sinatra forever. He had also had another child with Nancy, Frank Sinatra Jr. His life as a father and a supporter was constantly challenged by the unending adoration by thousands of young girls.

Girls were stealing pieces of his hair from barbers and wearing it around their necks in lockets—if he was lucky enough that they didn't try to pull it out of his actual head at appearances. After the Columbus Day Riot put to bed any idea that this would be a pleasant experience, Sinatra had to change the way that he approached living life, just to keep himself safe and sane.

A hallmark of the early Sinatramania years is the sheer volume in which Sinatra was forced to work. Even when he was just starting out, he was playing 6 shows a night at the Paramount. According to newspapers from the time, if a show was for 11 o'clock in the morning, the kids would start lining up at 11 o'clock the night before and wait all night for him to show up.

It was truly a ridiculous time and Sinatra's handlers and managers wanted to make sure that they capitalized on it. Around 1946, they decided that Frank should release his first album, called The Voice of Frank Sinatra. It was a short and tight little album that consisted of 8 tracks that Sinatra had released before. However, the album did fantastically. It was one of the first albums that would be registered on the Billboard pop music charts and it debuted at #1, staying there for nearly 2 months, starting in March 1946.

Sinatra was no slouch when he worked for Columbia records, recording multiple records and keeping them on the top of the charts for many, many months. His performance on "Sweet Lorraine", which also featured some prominent jazz musicians like Nat King Cole, was probably the artistic highlight of the era. During his heights, he was selling close to 10 million records a year.

He began to perform away from the stage, starring in a number of musicals that highlighted his incredible voice and tremendous animal magnetism. With On the Town, Sinatra starred in a musical that would be significant in the public consciousness for some time. He also had a popular radio show and several TV appearances.

However, all this activity and exposure was always bound to overload the circuits and come back down to Earth in one way or another. Sinatra was steadily losing his spot as the only male performer to really kick it off with the young girls. He had opened the floodgates, to be sure, but he was soon to find his arena would be flooded with his peers.

Not to mention, his family life was becoming more and more difficult to understand in the light of his massive popularity. So often, there are stars who begin their journey with a woman or man from their original echelon that they drag across time and space to the top of stardom. When they get there, though, the people want to see the real star, not the regular joe or jane. Nancy Sinatra was becoming more and more obsolete — especially when Sinatra had a public affair with Ava Gardner in 1947.

Sinatra began to receive more heat about his personal views. His previously benign progressivism based on his immigrant-like experiences was now seen as a fatal flaw by the half of the country that was sickened with the Red Fever. Anyone left of Joseph McCarthy could expect conservative publications to accuse them of everything but treason—and sometimes treason too. Sinatra was not immune, getting into an altercation with a columnist outside of a nightclub that resulted in Frank slugging the man who had accused him of Communism and anti-American activity.

Along with that, he was facing increasing scrutiny that his ties with the mob were nefarious and ill-conceived. He took trips to Havana, Cuba to see "Lucky" Luciano, a famous gangster, and attracted a great deal of heat for his connections to the old way. He was torn in two directions; his persona and his personality were clashing and it was unclear what he was going to end up as. Especially when you consider that, as his 3rd son was being birthed, he had his mind on actress Ava Gardner. His marriage was doomed. The Frank that everyone knew was dead and gone. Even he knew it.

When you play the game with the tenacity that Sinatra did, it will eventually catch up to you. He had spent his whole life searching for a way to live life as this person, yet, once he was that guy, he had no idea how to moderate himself. His sales started to suffer for many reasons. His voice was disintegrating on a daily basis. Given no chance to heal, his vocal chords were overworked and mangled to the point that he couldn't sing.

His relationship with a wild Hollywood starlet cut deep rivets into his reputation as a kind young man who was just talented enough to hit it big while supporting a family. His reputation started out as a heartthrob and was descending steadily to something more akin to the Greasers of the 50's and early 60's. As the young girls grew up, his fan base slowly dwindled.

By the time the 1950's came around, it was over for the first stage of Sinatra's life. MGM no longer wished to work with him. He divorced his wife, Nancy, and immediately married Ava Gardner—cementing his new role as the "big shot." He was the kind of person that would never have given his younger self the time of day. And as he was approaching 40 years old, he needed to find another way to connect with audiences and quickly.

One of his first choices, following his contentious and expensive divorce, was to head west to Las Vegas and try to capitalize on the budding market that was their entertainment scene. He, along with Dean Martin and Sammy Davis Jr., formed a group of entertainers that would come to define the Las Vegas scene for decades to come.

Their easy-going hedonism and remarkable chemistry was lauded extensively by the crowds that would center on the Vegas strip as it grew out of the desert in the 1950's. However glamorous this time may seem, Sinatra was at his lowest for the first couple of years in the new decade. He was a drunken, gambling mess that would consistently lose his voice because of intense emotional disturbance.

Once his manager and publicist died suddenly, there was not much that Sinatra could do to remain sane and he descended into a life that was as far away from the playful "pretend" honeymoon he had had a decade earlier could be. He owed money in taxes and was forced to borrow $200,000 from Columbia Records to stay afloat. He recorded his last record there in New York in 1952. Titled, "Why Try to Change Me Now", it was a somber recording — though quite good. It convinced a journalist to say about Sinatra," Sinatra had had it. It was sad. From the top to the bottom in one horrible lesson."

But Sinatra had one more trick up his sleeve. He had been reading a book titled From Here to Eternity and was certain that he could play a side character that was integral to the story. The thought consumed him. He wanted to make it back into the limelight and he wanted to do it on his own terms. He wasn't getting any younger and his dreams of becoming a performer had been fulfilled but in a way that was certainly unsatisfying. But first, he had to make himself respectable again.

He began to put himself back into his work, hoping that he could will himself into the minds of Americans again. He was recording and performing as often as possible and it finally seemed like he had found the groove that would allow him to be the successful long term. However, Colombia Records no longer wanted anything to do with him. He had to find a new recording company first.

There was a fledgling label that was just starting up that had Sinatra's eye. They were called Capitol records and they needed a big star to get their brand off the ground. The executives were impressed with the work that Sinatra had been putting in and felt that this could be their best opportunity to get recognition. Sinatra was signed to a lucrative 7-year deal.

To start with, he began recording some new songs for the label — for some reason, everything seemed to be turning around — these songs had all the pep and mysticism that his early material did. But there was something else, a knowing tone in his voice. This was the crowning of a man who had seen it all. He had gone from the bottom to the top and back down again. The comeback cannot be understated as one of the great American traditions and Sinatra began to embody it. When he heard the new sound fresh off the recording, he was entranced. Exclaiming, "I'm back, baby, I'm back!"

This song was entitled, "I've Got the World on a String" and it, somehow, perfectly encapsulated the feeling that Sinatra had about his comeback.

I've Got the World on a String
I've got the world on a string
I'm sitting on a rainbow
Got that string around my finger
What a world, what a life; I'm in love

I've got a song that I sing
And I can make the rain go
Anytime I move my finger
Lucky me, can't you see? I'm in love

Life's a wonderful thing
As long as I've got that string
I'd be a silly so-and-so
If I should ever let you go

I've got the world on a string
I'm sitting on the rainbow
I've got that string around my finger
Oh, what a world, what a life; I'm in love

Life's a wonderful thing
As long as I hold the string
I'd be a crazy so-and-so
If I should ever let her go

I've got the world on a string
I'm sitting on a rainbow
I got that string around my finger

Oh, what a world, what a life
Oh, what a world, what a life
What a world, what a life 'cause I'm in love
(He's in love, he's in love)

I'm in love

(Got the world on a string)
And what a wonderful thing
(All right)
When you get the world (Uh huh) on a string

Sinatra would then get the call that would cement his place in the pop culture echelon. He was invited to play the character he had been dreaming of in From Here to Eternity. Sinatra became the character on the big screen and stole back the hearts of the Americans who had loved him before. Before it was all said and done, Sinatra would win an Academy Award for the performance—becoming a critical darling and completing the daring comeback.

The End of an Era

The sign on the awning says, "From Here to Eternity." The little brick building in Hoboken's humble West End looks more like an old mortuary than a museum, and perhaps that's fitting.

For a few years, the place was a modest shrine to Frank Sinatra, the homegrown singer, and actor whose centennial is in December. He grew up in a tenement building next door, which burned down long ago. That small parcel is now a gravel parking lot used by a handful of Monroe Street residents, framed by a plain brick arch to mark the singer's birthplace.

--James Sullivan, Boston Globe, 2015

After he came back, Sinatra never left again. If you have any familiarity with American culture, you know him well. There is just no escaping the influence that he left in his wake. His career would run smoothly for, basically, the rest of his life. As he was laid to rest at the age of 82, he was respected, beloved, and imitated but never outshone.

Sinatra stayed with Capitol for a few years after his comeback but left again when he found that he would be better off setting his own schedule. He would go on to found Reprise Records in 1961 and stay on his own label for the next 20 years. Many would offer conjecture about the changes in his personality that made this possible. His time with the incredibly talented Sammy Davis Jr. likely changed the way he approached constructing a song. The Rat Pack, in general, was always a great resource to tap when he needed inspiration.

But, truthfully, the reason for his return to greatness is more than likely the return to his love of the craft. When he went back to what had worked for him before, the total immersion in the musical scene, it worked out for him as it had before. He would never be free of the political and personal squabbles that dominate the media coverage of Sinatra, but he would be free of his own self-doubts and misgivings.

It is not simply because of his fantastic talents that we remember him so fondly to this day. His story was one that inspired curiosity at every turn. There will never be another like him and there is no one else that represents the golden age of the United States quite so well. He was the light that the world followed and the voice that soothed it when things were bad. All while navigating the incredibly dense reality that he had crafted for himself — a poor immigrant's son from the wrong side of the Hudson.

Sinatra has the unique honor of being one of the only artists of his day to release successful albums and performances in the 40's, 50's, 60's, and 70's. For all the magic of the new era of music, he had staying power that was nearly unrivaled. Even Elvis struggled to balance the allure of wealth and fame with his own personal future over 30-40 years of fame.

His death would come almost at the dawn of the 21st century. He had legs for all of the 20th, but the world would have to go one alone without him for this new era. He died of a prolonged illness at the age of 82, the last fight, the only one he couldn't win.

When he died, the world wept with his family. The Empire State Building lit up blue for his blue eyes. The lights on the strip were dimmed in Vegas—something that was unheard of. They even stopped gambling for a moment—all to remember the greatest singer of the 20th century and possibly the greatest American entertainer of all time.

Printed in Great Britain
by Amazon